Let's Learn About Story Elements: Plot

Let's Learn About Story Elements: Plot
15 Creative Projects That Help Kids Become Better Readers and Writers

Michelle O'Brien-Palmer

illustrations by
Heidi Stephens

Credits

Cover Design: Jaime Lucero

Student Cover Art:
Nonfiction Shape Book: Nick Palmer
Story Cube: Caleb Garvin
Plot Viewer: Dan Williams & Derek Johnson

Content Editors:
Martha Ivy, teacher, Redmond, WA
Martha Ivy's 4th-grade students, Christa McAuliffe Elementary
Nancy Johnston, teacher, Woodinville, WA
Nancy Johnston's 6th-grade students, Wilder Elementary
Valerie Marshall, teacher, Redmond, WA
Valerie Marshall's 4th-grade students, Christa McAuliffe Elementary
Pam Schild, teacher, Woodinville, WA
Pam Schild's 6th-grade students, Wilder Elementary
Nancie Schonhard, teacher, Woodinville, WA
Nancie Schonhard's 6th-grade students, Wilder Elementary
Joyce Standing, teacher, Redmond, WA
Joyce Standing's students, The Overlake School

Other Contributors:
Stephanie Garcia, 6th-grade student, Wilder Elementary
Ann Lyman, teacher, Westhill Elementary
Julee Neupert, teacher, Ben Rush Elementary
Eileen Shaner, teacher, Franconia Elementary
Alesha Thomas, 6th-grade student, Wilder Elementary

Young Authors:

Kadi Anderson	Janet Kim	Sean O'Connor
Tierney Creech	Kristina Lin	Nick Palmer
Emily Gibbons	Justin Lobdell	Brian Schnierer
Meghan Gibbons	Matt Marcoe	Broderick Smith
Lisa Hails	Andy Meade	Sandy Stonesifer
Jenny Jones	Willie Nelson	Christi Warren
		Jackie White

ISBN 0-590-10716-X

Copyright © 1998 by Michelle O'Brien-Palmer. All rights reserved.

Text sections originally published as part of I Love to Read copyright © 1995 by Michelle O'Brien-Palmer

Printed in the U.S.A.

Acknowledgments

I would like to thank the following people for their support and contributions in the creation of *Let's Learn About Story Elements: Plot*.

I am especially grateful to the 6th-grade editors for your honest feedback, project recommendations and inspiration for this book. In our seven months together, you made significant contributions in molding *Let's Learn About Story Elements: Plot* into its final form. I am very proud to have had the opportunity to work through the writing process with you as my editors.

- Thanks to the student editors from Nancy Johnston's class at Wilder Elementary School. Your project ideas and examples were wonderful. I really appreciate your sharing them with the readers of this book.
- Thanks to the student editors from Pam Schild's class at Wilder Elementary School. Your responsible attitude and great ideas really made a difference in this book.
- Thanks to the student editors from Nancie Schonhard's class at Wilder Elementary School. Your suggestions for materials, material lists, and organizing forms will help the readers of this book immensely.

I also extend sincere thanks to those who helped in the production of this book:

To the young authors for their project examples – Kadi Anderson, Eunice Chung, Tierney Creech, Carey DeAngelis, Colby Emerson, Emily Gibbons, Hannah Gibbons, Meghan Gibbons, Lisa Hails, Billy Harris, Jenny Jones, Janet Kim, Kristina Lin, Justin Lobdell, Edward Lobdell, Greg Lundwall, Matt Marcoe, Andy Meade, Willie Neslon, Tara O'Brien, Sean O'Connor, Nick Palmer, Brian Schnierer, Broderick Smith, Sandy Stonesifer, Michael Strong, Terry Yoo, Steven Yoo, Christi Warren, Jamie Weaver, and Jackie White. To Stephanie Garcia and Alesha Thomas for their great project ideas.

To Valerie Marshall and Martha Ivy's students at McAuliffe Elementary – thank you for inviting me into your classroom. I had such fun talking with you and sharing the process of writing this book. I really appreciate the special effort you made to help me problem solve.

To Joyce Standing's students at The Overlake School – you are so enthusiastic and excited about reading and writing it was inspiring to be among you. Thank you for sharing your projects.

To Martha Ivy, Ann Lyman, Nancy Johnston, Valerie Marshall, Julee Neupert, Eileen Shaner, Pam Schild, Nancie Schonhard, and Joyce Standing for sharing your project ideas.

To Heidi Stephens for your wonderfully inspired illustrations. To Peg Kehret for her wonderful support as my mentor and friend.

To my husband, Gid Palmer for your constant support through my creative adventures and to my son, Nick Palmer for your willingness to stop everything to produce a writing sample. To Evelyn Sansky for a lifetime of friendship, and to Marcene and Bob Christoverson for their ongoing support of my work.

Let's Learn About Story Elements: Plot
is **dedicated** to every child involved in this book

Nancie Schonhard's Students

Zach Barth
Samson Chiang
T.C. Colleran
Tierney Creech
Reggie Green
Jay Hellenga
Jenny Jones
P.J. Kapsales
Dustin Marshall

Justin Matts
Luke Myers

David Stolowitz
Jackie White

Joyce Standing's Students

Michelle Bauer
Eunice Chung
Colby Emerson
Billy Harris
Diane Jenkins
Peter Johnson
Kristina Lin
Matt Marcoe
Mark Mavis

Andy Meade
Darcy Milne
Broderick Smith
Shon Smith
Sandy Stonesifer
Kacie Tomlinson
Evan Tuck
Chrissy Wakeling
Jamie Weaver

Valerie Marshall and

Taylor Bass
Dana Bentsen
Andrew Blair
Meghan Blume
Bernie Boglioli
Kaitlyn Bolduc
Jamie Boscow
Chris Brown
Carey Cade
Kaitlin Carbrey
Michael Chealander
Annie Chiu
Julie Culleton
Jordan Davidoff
Jennifer Dickens
Stephanie Diers

Matt Farrington
Andrea Geary
Justin Gedney
Meryl Goodwin
Matthew Hecker
Brady Johnson
Jenny Keaton
Matthew Kesl
Shawn Kidd
Michael Kilburg
Megan Kilkelly
Melissa Kowalchuk
Jessee Kubitz
Nick Landi
Brian Leierzapf
Sean Logue

Katharine Mackey
Elise McKinney
Vimombi Nshom
Pat O'Leary
Jeremy Peronto
Casey Peterson
Nick Ramsey
Robert Reimer
Katie Rooney
Ryan Shane
Kelsey Sikma
Stephanie Sinclair
Michael Slaughter
Conor Thurman
Jake Vela
Erin Whittington
Kaitlin Wight

and Martha Ivy's Students

Pam Schild and Nancy Johnston's Students

Kadi Anderson
Nathan Belt
Melissa Bernard
Cassie Bolin
Carey DeAngelis
Caitlin Endres
Stephanie Garcia
Jessica Gregson
Lisa Hails

Jeff Hill
Janet Kim
Greg Lundwall
Willie Nelson
Sean O'Connor
Krissy Shea
Michael Strong
Craig Swanson
Alesha Thomas
Christi Warren

Young Authors

Kadi Anderson
Tierney Creech
Emily Gibbons
Meghan Gibbons
Lisa Hails
Jenny Jones
Janet Kim
Kristina Lin
Justin Lobdell
Matt Marcoe
Andy Meade
Willie Nelson
Sean O'Connor
Nick Palmer
Brian Schnierer
Broderick Smith
Sandy Stonesifer
Christi Warren
Jackie White

Table of Contents

Introduction
for Parents and Teachers

Let's Learn About Story Elements: Plot was written to give children (2nd-5th grade) an enticing selection of reading extension projects focused on the story element of plot. Each project was chosen by other kids as one they would especially recommend. This text is part of the Let's Learn About Story Elements series, which includes books on character and setting.

Although the text speaks to children directly, it will require adult supervision and guidance in most cases. There are projects which require an Exacto™ knife, scissors and sometimes other potentially dangerous appliances. Each chapter includes front pages with a visual representation of the chapter contents. This is to help children visually identify those experiences which are of interest to them. Whenever extra information might be helpful to parents or teachers, it will be found in italics just under the project head. The second chapter (Keeping Track) includes organizing forms for books, projects and materials. There are also forms throughout the text that you may copy for use in your classroom. The reference list at the end of Chapter Two is intended to provide a number of excellent resources for bringing literature into your home or classroom.

Each project idea in this book is meant to be taken as liberally as possible. There is no one right way to do any project. The more variations created, the more exciting the process will be.

Foreword to Kids

I love to read! The kids who helped me write this book love reading too. We decided to create three books which celebrate reading and share some of our favorite reading projects with you. We worked together for seven months in a school library which looks much like the illustration on page 5; we shared project ideas, tested those ideas, and finally came up with our list of favorite projects related to plot. We hope you enjoy these projects as much as we do.

The chapter, Keeping Track, was designed to help you organize your project materials and keep track of the books you read and the projects you complete. You can copy these forms and use them to gather your project supplies.

Some projects will be new to you and some may be similar to projects you've made before. Use your imagination to create your own unique projects.

Have fun celebrating your favorite books!

I Love to Read

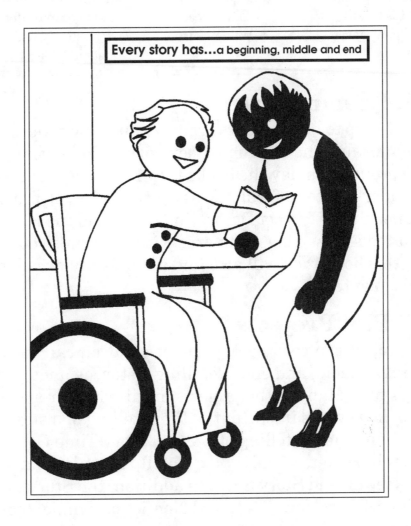

Every story has...a beginning, middle and end

Chapter 1

Introduction

This chapter provides a brief introduction to each main chapter. *Let's Learn About Story Elements: Plot* was written with the help of over 100 kids. They were part of the writing and editing process. The young authors who share their unedited project examples in the book are listed below:

Kadi Anderson	Janet Kim	Sean O'Connor
Tierney Creech	Kristina Lin	Nick Palmer
Emily Gibbons	Justin Lobdell	Brian Schnierer
Meghan Gibbons	Matt Marcoe	Broderick Smith
Lisa Hails	Andy Meade	Sandy Stonesifer
Jenny Jones	Willie Nelson	Christi Warren
		Jackie White

Chapter 2: Keeping Track

This chapter is set up to help readers organize and track their books, projects, and project materials. The Reading Bookworm allows younger readers an opportunity to proudly display the books they have read. The Track-a-Project Sheet gives readers instant feedback as to the types of projects they have created. The Checklist of Project Decorating Items and the Plot Project Supply Sheet are great tools for setting up an area with materials you'll need to create the projects in this book. You will also find a number of excellent resources at the back of this chapter.

Chapter 3: Plot Projects

The first plot project is a card book younger children can make to identify a story's beginning, middle, and end. Retelling a story is another way of identifying the story's plot. Many of the projects in this chapter are based upon the identification of key events important in the retelling of a story. The following projects will enhance any retelling of a story; Story Time Capsule, Story Pop-Out, Story Retell Poster, Candy Box Retell, First-Person Journal, Story Banner, Story Viewer, and Story Sack. In addition, the Story Pop-Out, Fold-a-Story, Story Cube, Story Newsletter and Nonfiction Shape Book can all stand alone as alternatives to standard book reports.

Chapter 4: Project Recipes

This chapter includes how-tos for making different project materials like modeling clay and sewn books.

Keeping Track

Chapter 2

To Help You Keep Track...

Project Organizers

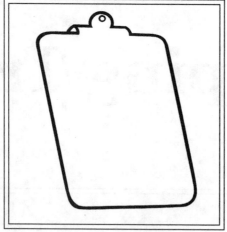

page 15 – page 17

Reading Bookworm

page 18 – page 19

Track-a-Project Sheet

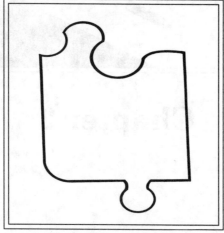

page 20 – page 21

I LOVE TO READ

Plot Project List

Name:_____

Date: _____

Select one of the following book projects to share with your class:

- ❑ **Beginning, Middle & End Book**
- ❑ **Story Time Capsule**
- ❑ **Story Pop-Out**
- ❑ **Fold-a-Story**
- ❑ **Story Cube Pop-Up**
- ❑ **Story Retell Poster**
- ❑ **Cereal Box Theatre**
- ❑ **Story Newsletter**
- ❑ **Candy Box Retell**
- ❑ **First-Person Journal**
- ❑ **Nonfiction Shape Book**
- ❑ **Story Banner**
- ❑ **Guess the Character Book**
- ❑ **Story Viewer**
- ❑ **Story Sack Retell**

Checklist of Project Decorating Items

- [ ] aluminum foil
- [ ] beads
- [ ] beans
- [ ] bottle caps
- [ ] brass fasteners
- [ ] buttons
- [ ] cans
- [ ] cardboard
- [ ] cardboard tubes
- [ ] clay
- [ ] colored moss
- [ ] colored paper
- [ ] colored pencils
- [ ] colored plastic wrap
- [ ] computer paper
- [ ] construction paper
- [ ] cookie cutters
- [ ] cotton balls (colored)
- [ ] cotton swabs
- [ ] crepe paper
- [ ] drinking straws
- [ ] egg cartons
- [ ] fabric paint
- [ ] fabric scraps
- [ ] feathers
- [ ] felt squares
- [ ] film containers
- [ ] finger paints
- [ ] glitter
- [ ] glue stick
- [ ] googly eyes
- [ ] hangers
- [ ] lace
- [ ] magazines
- [ ] margarine tubs

- [ ] markers
- [ ] milk cartons
- [ ] newspapers
- [ ] plain paper
- [ ] paper clips
- [ ] paper cups
- [ ] paper plates
- [ ] paper scraps
- [ ] pastels
- [ ] pie tins
- [ ] pipe cleaners
- [ ] popsicle sticks
- [ ] ribbon
- [ ] sand
- [ ] shells
- [ ] spices
- [ ] sponges
- [ ] spools
- [ ] stickers
- [ ] string
- [ ] tagboard pieces
- [ ] tissue paper
- [ ] toothpicks
- [ ] twigs
- [ ] wallpaper pieces
- [ ] wire
- [ ] wood scraps
- [ ] wrapping paper
- [ ] yarn
- [ ] _____
- [ ] _____
- [ ] _____
- [ ] _____
- [ ] _____
- [ ] _____
- [ ] _____

Plot Project Supplies

☆My Plot Project Supply Sheet

Name:

My Project is:_____

To do my project I will need:

___ Recipe: _____

    page #:_____

Writing Tools

___ pencil(s)

___ marker(s)

___ pen(s)

___ crayons

Art Supplies

___ glue

___ paste

___ scissors

___ paint

___ paint brush

___ glitter

___ stickers

___ tape

___ clay

___ Exacto™ knife

___ ruler

Paper Supplies

___ form: page #____

___ plain paper

___ lined paper

___ construction paper

___ craft paper

___ tagboard

___ cardboard

___ shelf paper

___ index card

___ _____

___ _____

Other Possible Items

___ book

___ shoe box

___ reference books

___ hole punch

___ cereal box

___ computer/printer

___ gift box

___ candy box

___ cardboard box

___ hole punch

___ plastic sewing needle

___ yarn/cord

___ coat hanger

___ stapler

___ paper towel tubes

Reading Bookworm

A reading bookworm is another way to record the books you've read. Primary grade children love this project.

Materials:
Colored cardstock
Scissors
Page 19
Hole punch
Laminating materials
O-Ring

Goal:
To keep track of the books you've read.

Steps:
1. Copy the bookworm form on colored cardstock.
2. Cut out one of the bookworms.
3. Write your name, the book title and the date you finished reading the book inside the bookworm.
4. Laminate the bookworm.
5. Punch a hole in the eye section.
6. Place your completed bookworm on an O-ring.
7. Each time you read a book fill out a worm.
8. Share your reading bookworms with your friends.

Bookworm Form

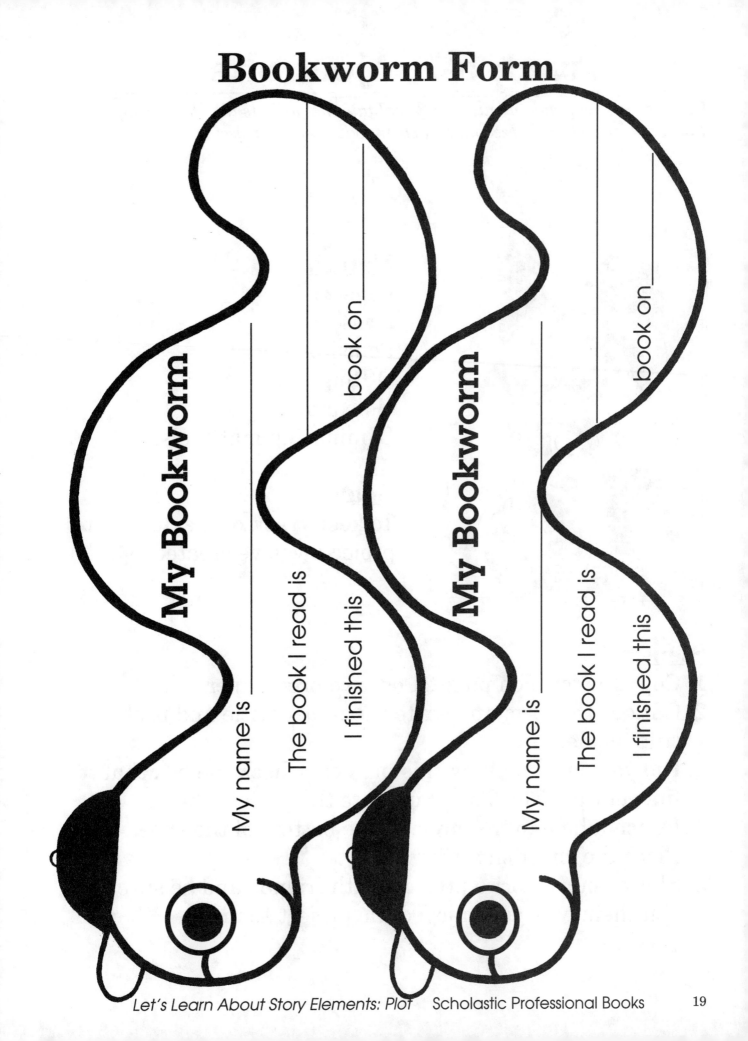

My Bookworm

My name is _____

The book I read is _____

I finished this _____ book on _____

My Bookworm

My name is _____

The book I read is _____

I finished this _____ book on _____

Track-a-Project Sheet

These sheets help kids monitor and evaluate the projects they have completed. For fast tracking, kids recommend color coding each project.

Materials:
Page 21
Scissors
Pencil/pen
O-Ring
Hole punch
Laminating materials

Goal:
To keep track of the different projects you've created.

Steps:
1. Copy the form on page 21 onto colored paper.
2. Cut out the form and write the project title and book title inside.
3. Did you enjoy making this project? Check the box that fits your answer. Then laminate the project sheet.
4. Punch a hole in the circle at the bottom of the sheet. Place the sheet on a ring.
5. Share your favorite projects with friends and be sure to tell them why you enjoyed the project so much.

Plot Project Sheet

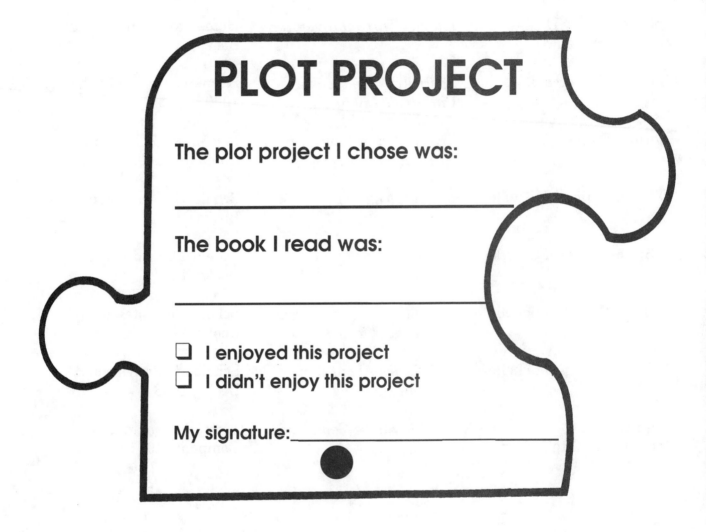

PLOT PROJECT

The plot project I chose was:

_____

The book I read was:

_____

❑ I enjoyed this project
❑ I didn't enjoy this project

My signature:_____

Reference Books

Author	Book Title	Publisher
Brown, Hazel Cambourne, Brian	*Read and Retell*	Heinemann Educational Books, 1990
Calkins, Lucy McCormick	*Lessons From a Child*	Heinemann Educational Books, 1986
Johnson, Terry D. Louis, Daphne R.	*Literacy Through Literature*	Heinemann Educational Books, 1987
Luekens, Rebecca J.	*A Critical Handbook of Children's Literature*	HarperCollins Publishers, 1990
Norton, Donna	*The Impact of Literature-Based Reading*	Macmillan Publishing Company, 1992
O'Brien-Palmer, Michelle	*Beyond Book Reports*	Scholastic Professional Books, 1997
O'Brien-Palmer, Michelle	*Great Graphic Organizers*	Scholastic Professional Books, 1997
O'Brien-Palmer, Michelle	*Let's Learn About Story Elements: Character*	Scholastic Professional Books, 1998
O'Brien-Palmer, Michelle	*Let's Learn About Story Elements: Setting*	Scholastic Professional Books, 1998
Rothlein, Liz Meinbach, Anita Meyer	*The Literature Connection*	Scott, Foresman and Company, 1991

Plot Projects

Chapter 3

Chapter Contents

The plot is how the story goes; the problems and solutions the author shows.

Stories can surprise you as they twist and turn, teaching us lessons the characters learn.

Beginning, Middle & End Book

Story Time Capsule

Story Pop-Out

Fold-a-Story

Today's Fold-a-Story
Deep Trouble
by Franklin W. Dixon

Characters

Plot
Setting

Conflict

Story Cube Pop-Up

Story Retell Poster

Brian~Hatchet

Chapter Contents

Cereal Box Theater

page 38

Story Newsletter

page 40

Candy Box Retell

page 42

First-Person Journal

page 44

Nonfiction Shape Book

page 46

Story Banner

page 48

Guess the Character Book

page 50

Story Viewer

page 52

Story Sack Retell

page 54

Beginning, Middle & End Book

The Beginning, Middle & End Book is a fun introduction to plot for younger children. The written information can be dictated.

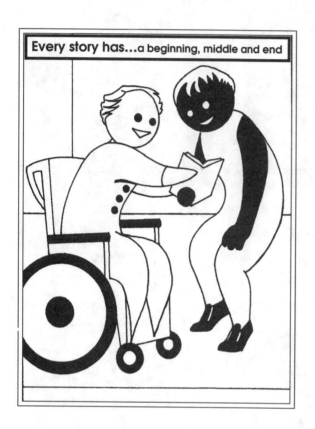

Every story has...a beginning, middle and end

Materials:
Pencil(s)/markers
Page 56 and page 59

Goal:
To identify a story's beginning, middle and end.

Steps:
1. Copy the form on page 56. Follow the directions for the card book on page 59.
2. Draw a picture of your favorite character on the front cover.
3. On the first page of your book, draw what happened at the beginning of the story.
4. On the next page, draw what happened in the middle of the story.
5. On the last page, draw what happened at the end of the story.

Beginning, Middle & End Book Example

My Beginning, Middle, and End Book

My Favorite Character

Story: Dance at Grandpas
My name: Justin Lobdell

Book Cover

This happened in the **beginning**...

In the beginning baby Carie and her sister and her mom and dad are going to their grandpas on a a horse pulling a sled.

First Page

This happened in the **middle**...

In the middle, their grandpa was changing all the babies diapers.

Second Page

This happened in the **end**...

At the very, very end, everybody at Grandpa's house is dancing.

Back Page

Story Time Capsule

The students in Nancie Schonhard's classroom at Wilder Elementary had a wonderful time creating unique time capsules for the books they were reading. Three of their projects are shown on the next page. This is a very open-ended project.

Materials:
Recycled items
Markers/pens
Paint
Glue

Goal:
To create a time capsule for a story.

Steps:
1. Close your eyes and imagine you are one of the characters in the story.
2. Write a list of items you would include in a time capsule which would tell others about your life as this character.
3. Decide upon the actual form of the time capsule (see examples on page 29). Make sure it relates to the story in some way.
4. Collect items you will need for the inside.
5. Make your time capsule and place the story items inside.
6. Share your time capsule with friends.

Story Time Capsule Examples

King of the Wind
project created by Jenny Jones

Summer of the Swans
project created by Tierney Creech

Bridge to Terabithia
project created by Jackie White

Story Pop-Out

Stefanie Garcia, a 6th-grader at Wilder Elementary, highly recommends this project for kids of all ages. The Story Pop-Out can be used as a unique book report or interesting presentation starter.

Materials:
Construction paper
(18-by-12 inches)
Scissors
Pencil/crayons
Glue

Goal:
To create a house from a story and use it to retell the story.

Steps:

1. Fold two sides of a sheet of construction paper into the middle.
2. Cut the top in the shape of a roof (see page 31).
3. Draw a character and write the title, author, and your name on the cover.
4. Cut a large door and two windows out of construction paper scraps. Glue them to the inside of the house shape so that they can open and close.
5. Write the story summary and character information on the inside panels.
6. Draw characters in the windows and door.

Story Pop-Out Directions

Steps 1 and 2
(18-by-12 inches)

Step 3

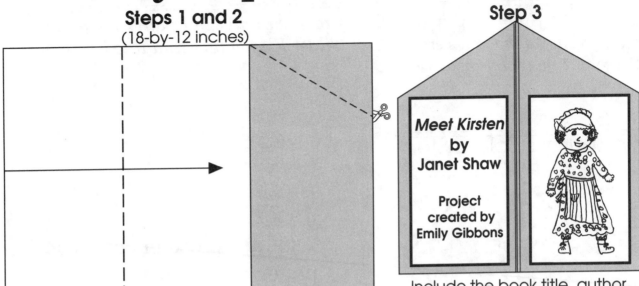

Fold two sides of construction paper into the middle. Cut each side at an angle to form a peak.

Include the book title, author, your name and a picture of the character.

Step 4

Cut a large door and two windows out of construction paper. Glue them to the inside of the house shape.

Step 5

The main character in this story is Kirsten. Kirsten is Swedish. She's a Viking. She is nice. She has blonde hair. She wears her hair in braids looped up. She is 9 years old and she lives with her cousins.

Write a story summary and information about your favorite character on the inside panels.

Step 6

Story Summary
Kirsten was from Sweden. Her family traveled on a boat to get to America. Her friend, Marta, was with them and she died from a fever on the boat.

When Kirsten got to America she was following her dad and her brother, Peter to get some milk and she got lost. She was very scared. A nice lady found her and took her back.

Then she lived with her cousins, Anna and Lisbeth. She thought they were very kind and liked playing with them.

Story Characters
The main character in this story is Kirsten. Kirsten is Swedish. She's a Viking. She is nice. She has blonde hair. She wears her hair in braids looped up. She is 9 years old and she lives with her cousins.

Another character is Anna. She's Kirsten's cousin. She has blonde hair too, but she was born in America. She is nice to Kirsten.

Lisbeth is Anna's sister. She has brownish hair. She's older than Kirsten. She acts more grown up than Kirsten and Anna.

Draw characters in the windows and door.

Fold-a-Story

The Fold-a-Story is open-ended, easy to make and can be adjusted for all ages. Nancy Johnston's students at Wilder Elementary find it to be a great presentation tool or book report.

Materials:
A square piece of construction paper
Pencil/pens/markers

Goal:
To identify key elements in a story.

Steps:
1. Fold construction paper in half to create two triangles.
2. Fold top and bottom corners to the center.
3. Fold the remaining sides to form a square.
4. Write story information on the four external sides. The front of the project can include your name, the date, the book title and author, and other interesting information.
5. You may want to draw a story scene on the inside square and include information on setting, plot, characters, and main conflict on each flap.
6. Pop open your square to reveal the story.

Fold-a-Story Directions

Step 1

Fold construction paper in half, to form two triangles.

Step 2

Fold two corners to the center fold.

Step 3

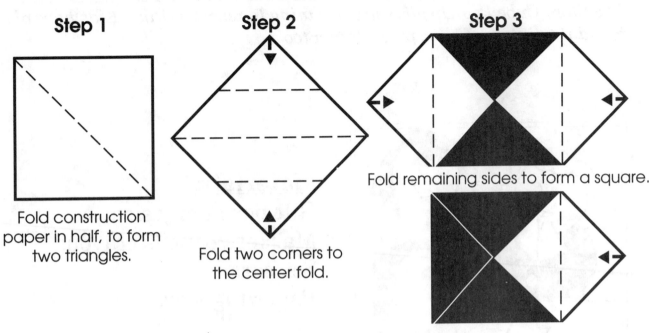

Fold remaining sides to form a square.

Step 4

Write story information on four sides of the outside as shown.

Sean O'Connor
October 2, 1994

Hardy Boys Casefiles #54 Deep Trouble by Franklin W. Dixon

Frank and Joe Hardy travel to the Bahamas for fortune and glory but that's not all they find.

Have you ever read a book with car chases, shoot-outs, sharks, mystery, treasure, and boats on fire? If you haven't read this book, I doubt you have.

Sample

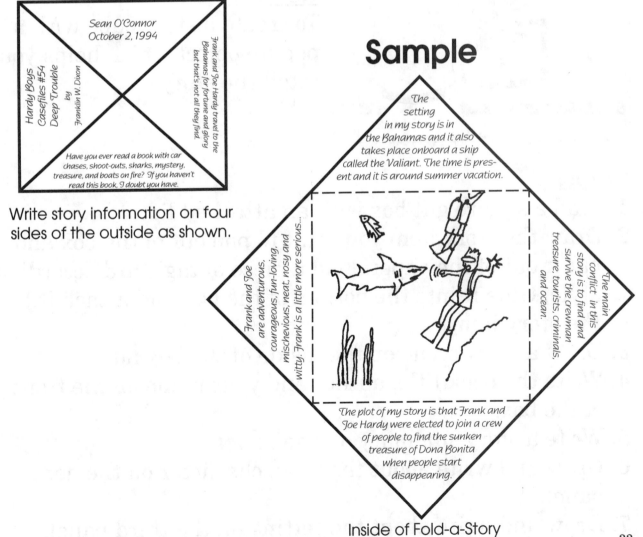

The setting in my story is in the Bahamas and it also takes place onboard a ship called the Valiant. The time is present and it is around summer vacation.

Frank and Joe are adventurous, courageous, fun-loving, mischevious, neat, nosy and witty. Frank is a little more serious...

The main conflict in this story is to find and survive the crewman treasure, tourists, criminals, and ocean.

The plot of my story is that Frank and Joe Hardy were elected to join a crew of people to find the sunken treasure of Dona Bonita when people start disappearing.

Inside of Fold-a-Story

Story Cube Pop-Up

The Story Cube Pop-Up gives new meaning to report writing. Kids have also found it to be an effective presentation tool.

Materials:
Gift box of any size
Markers/pencils/crayons
Scissors
Paper/tagboard

Goal:
To create a story cube with a pop-up object which helps you retell the story.

Steps:
1. Find a square gift box with an attached lid.
2. Draw the story item you want to pop out of the box and cut it out of the paper. Fold a piece of tagboard accordion style. Glue it into the bottom of the box and attach it to the story item.
3. Draw a story scene on the inside of the box lid.
4. Write the book title, author and your name on the front of the box.
5. Write a story summary on one panel.
6. Draw and write about the main character on the next panel.
7. Draw and write about the setting on the third panel.

Story Cube Pop-Up Example

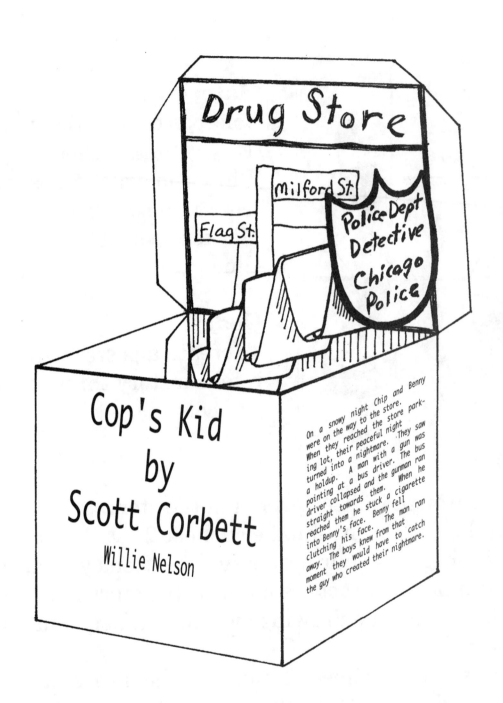

Drug Store

Milford St.

Flag St.

Police Dept
Detective

Chicago
Police

Cop's Kid
by
Scott Corbett

Willie Nelson

On a snowy night Chip and Benny were on the way to the store. When they reached the store parking lot, their peaceful night turned into a nightmare. They saw a holdup. A man with a gun was pointing at a bus driver. The bus driver collapsed and the gunman ran straight towards them. When he reached them he stuck a cigarette into Benny's face. Benny fell clutching his face. The man ran away. The boys knew from that moment they would have to catch the guy who created their nightmare.

Story Retell Poster

A story retell poster captures critical story elements through representative symbols. The poster can become the foundation for a book-talk or a story retell.

Materials:
Colored construction paper (17-by-12 inches) - sheet 1
White construction paper (12-by-9 inches) - sheet 2
Markers/pencils
Glue

Goal:
To create a poster which retells a story through story symbols.

Steps:
1. Think through the key events in the story.
2. Write the title in the middle of sheet 2.
3. Using sheet 2 as your poster surface, focus your drawings around a character's name or the story title. Remember to include drawings which will help you retell the story.
4. Center sheet 2 on sheet 1 and glue them together.
5. Use your drawing to retell the story to a friend or your classmates.

Story Retell Poster Example

Retell by Christi Warren

Cereal Box Theater

Kids love to act out the stories they've read. The Cereal Box Theater works well with all kinds of story character puppets. It may require adult supervision and help with cutting.

Materials:
Scissors/Exacto™ knife
Markers
Shelf paper/wallpaper
Large cereal box

Goal:
To create a theater for story retellings.

Steps:

1. Take the liner out of an empty cereal box. Cut off both sides and the back of the box.
2. Cut a rectangle out of the front of the box.
3. Select shelf paper to cover the box. Place the box on top of the paper's sticky side, leaving a one-inch border.
4. Cut a V shape above and below the box's fold lines. Cut out squares in each corner and fold the paper over so it covers the box.
5. Cut the hole out of the shelf paper.
6. Turn the theater over and use it as a prop for the retelling of a story.

Cereal Box Theater Directions

Step 1

Take the plastic liner out of an empty cereal box. Cut off both sides and the back.

Step 2

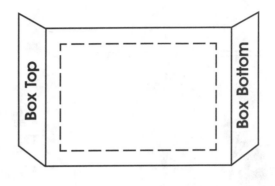

Use an Exacto knife™ to cut a rectangle out of the front side of the cereal box.

Step 3

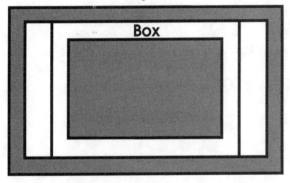

Select shelf paper to cover the cut out cereal box. Leave at least an inch around the outside. Place the box on top of the shelf paper's sticky side.

Step 4

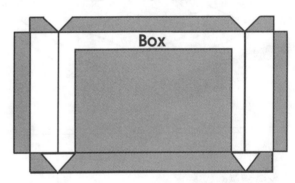

Cut a V shape above and below the fold lines. Cut out squares in each corner. Fold the paper over.

Step 5

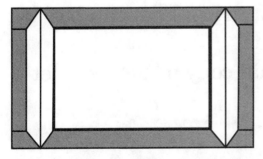

After you've folded the shelf paper over, cut the hole out with an Exacto™ knife.

Step 6

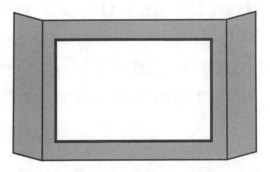

Turn the theater over and use it in the retelling of a story.

Story Newsletter

The Story Newsletter can take many forms, as shown in the individual and partner examples from Joyce Standing's students.

Materials:
Paper
Pencil/markers
Computer (optional)
Printer (optional)
Newsletter software (optional)

Goal:
To create a newsletter based upon a story's plot.

Steps:
1. Select a book you will use for the newsletter.
2. Think about the reader. What story information do you want your newsletter to give?
3. Make a list of questions you want to answer in this newsletter.
4. Use the questions to create a first draft. This can be written on a computer or by hand.
5. Revise, edit and then create a final copy of the newsletter to share with your friends.

Story Newsletter Examples
Newsletters based on the book
From the Mixed Up Files of Mrs. Basil E. Frankweiler

Newsletter created by Broderick Smith and Matt Marcoe

The Smarcoe Times
Missing Since Friday

A tragic event took place on a Friday in November. A young boy named Jamie and a young girl named Claudia stepped into there school bus and never returned home. They have both been missing for a week now. The kids parents are offering a large amount of money to the person who can provide a clue which could lead to where these kids have gone. People have been making anominous tips which are so far leading to nothing at all. If these kids have been seen or you know where they are please call 999-9631.

This is a recent family photo.

Jamie - Claudia

Strange sightings in the metropolitan museum.

Recently the metropolitan museum night watch guards have been reporting strange people walking around the old musuem. On watchmen indicated that in pursuit of the figures they will slowly fade away. Another watchman on duty said that he found a young boy

about 9 years old in the bathroom. The guard was scared be
an
see
in t
mu
yo

Newsletter created by Sandy Stonesifer

Angel By Michelangelo
by Sandy Stonesifer

THE WEEKLY HERALD

Your Mailbox
by Sandy Stonesifer

This angel is from the Metropolitan Museum of art. It was sold to the museum for $225 by Mrs. Basil E. Frankweiler. She has a private collection that is very large. It used to be kept at her house in New York but that house was closed. The museum's scientists are looking at the statue to determine whether it was done by Michelangelo or not. Their strongest clue remains the M engraved at he base of the statue. This large M is considered a stone mason's mark. Mrs. Frankweiler has told the scientists

Missing
by Sandy Stonesifer

Claudia and Jamie Kincaid are from Greenwich New York. They have been gone for two days. Their parents are frantic. They never arrived at school. The police have ruled out kidnapping because Claudia left a note saying not to worry. Claudia is twelve years old and Jamie eight. They are believed to be somewhere in New York city.

Page 1

The Post Office on Martin street's mailboxes are all filled up. The last available mailbox was bought yesterday for approximately four dollars a quarter. Why are all of a sudden so many people buying mailboxes? Well, Sam, a postal worker, says there are more houses that don't have mailboxes now.

Candy Box Retell

Eileen Shaner's students at Franconia Elementary in Souderton, PA enjoy using her book in a box idea. When the box is opened, the story unfolds. This is a great presentation starter.

Materials:
Ruler
Markers/pen(s)
Construction paper
Tape
Candy box
Scissors

Goal:
To create a story summary that can be folded into a fun, decorated box.

Steps:

1. Select the story you want to retell.
2. Determine how many pages you will have in your summary (see example on page 43).
3. Measure the box and cut out the pages.
4. Create a title page on the first page. Draw story events on the remaining pages.
5. Use the top of the box to create the book cover.
6. Glue the back side of the title page to the box cover.
7. Tape the pages together accordion style.
8. Fold the pages into the box.
9. Use your candy box to retell the story to your friends.

Candy Box Retell Directions

Steps 1 and 2

Select the story you want to retell. Decide what you want to include in your retell (words and pictures).

Step 3

Measure your box and cut out the number of pages you will need to complete your retell.

Step 4

Create your story retell on the pages you've cut.

Step 5

Decorate the top of the box as a book cover.

Sample

A Little Princess

project
by
Meghan Gibbons

Glue the back of the first page to the box cover, then tape the pages together like an accordion. Fold the pages inside the box and share your project with friends.

First-Person Journal

Martha Ivy and Valerie Marshall use their First-Person Journal idea with students in their literature circles. Journal writing is an effective way to write and react from the character's perspective.

Materials:
2 tagboard pieces
(5 1/2-by-4 1/4 inches)
4-5 sheets of paper
Markers/pencils
Hole punch
Page 60

Goal:
To keep a journal in which you write as if you were the character in a story.

Steps:
1. Choose the character you want to be in your journal.
2. Follow the steps on page 60 to make a sewn book.
3. Each time you read the book, write in your journal. You can tell about specific events and share your thoughts and feelings.
4. Decorate the book cover. You can make it plain or festive. For fun, try decorating the cover with items you really liked in the story.
5. Share your journal with friends.

First-Person Journal Example

My Diary

Peter

Number the Stars

written by

Nick Palmer

Today I saw Annemarie and Kristi. It was nice to see them. They remind me of Lisa. I gave them presents and gave their parents a resistance paper. I am worried about soldiers who stopped them on the street.

I'm working on a plan to save Ellen and her parents. The soldiers have trained dogs to find humans. This makes my work more dangerous. So scientists are making a scent to make the dog's sense of smell go away for a few hours.

Nonfiction Shape Book

Shape books can be used as an alternative to reports. They can also provide a format for giving a presentation in class. Joyce Standing's students used a number of reference books on a topic to create their shape books.

Materials:
Construction paper
White paper
Pens/markers
Stapler
Reference books

Goal:
To record information collected through research.

Steps:

1. Based on the information you've read, decide upon the shape of your book.
2. List the things you want to include in your book (topics).
3. Cut the cover out of construction paper and cut the pages out of paper.
4. Decorate your cover and write your information on the pages.
5. Staple the cover and pages together.
6. Share your book with friends.

Nonfiction Shape Book

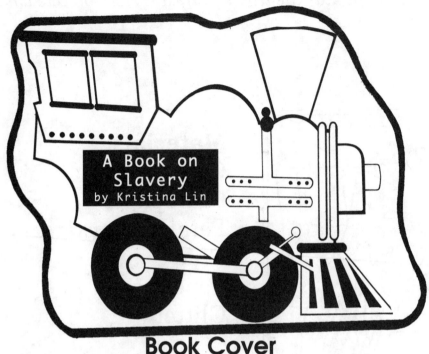

A Book on
Slavery
by Kristina Lin

Book Cover

Rebellion
  Many slaves tried to fight against
slavery. Some of them led rebellions.
      Nat Turner: He was a slave in
 Virginia that led a rebellion in 1831.
He and other slaves tried to escape.In
most rebellions the leaders and most of the
slaves were caught and killed.
What they didn't have
   Slaves didn't have mush of a choice on how
    they lived. They didn't g
     to public schools, or ow
     had to get their owners
   sion to leave the plantic
to have permission from th
get married.

Work
  Most of the slaves worked on cotton
plantions int the South. It was in the
United States from 1800 to 1860. Some
slaves worked in the house of white
slave owners. They cooked,cleaned and
.ıelped take care of the slaveowners children, but many of the slaves did planting,
raising,and harvesting crops.The slaves in the
fields worked from sunrise to sunset.
Living Quarters
     Families lived in different huts. There
     were no bedsteads or furniture.The beds
     were made of straw and old rags.The own-
     ers provided their slaves with the houses
     they lived in,food they ate,and the clothes
     they wore.

Story Banner

The Story Banner helps kids identify significant story objects when giving a book-talk.

Materials:
Coat hanger
Craft paper
Paint or markers
Glue
Paper/pencil
Glitter

Goal:
To create a banner that uses symbols to represent import- ant story events.

Steps:
1. Think through the story you have selected and make a list of five important story events. Choose an object (symbol) to represent each event.
2. Draw a draft of your banner on paper.
3. Cut craft paper to fit the width of a hanger.
4. Fold the paper through the hanger and glue the overlap to the back of the sheet as shown in step 4.
5. Create your banner with paint or markers.
6. Hang your story banner and retell the story to friends.

Story Banner Directions

Steps 1 and 2

Think through the story and list five important events. Draw objects (symbols) which represent each event. Draw a draft of your banner.

Step 3

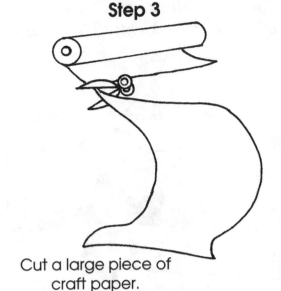

Cut a large piece of craft paper.

Step 4

Fold the paper through the hanger and glue it to itself.

Sample

father's hat & book by Janet Kim

The chimney & bird cage by Kadi Anderson

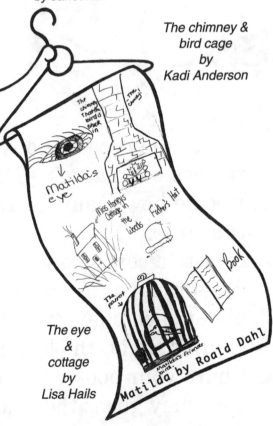

The eye & cottage by Lisa Hails

Step 5

Create your banner with paint or markers.

Hang your story banner and retell the story to your friends.

Guess the Character Book

Joyce Standing's students enjoyed sharing their Guess the Character Books with fellow students. This project can be easily tailored to all ages.

Materials:
Markers/pencils
Pages 59–61

Goal:
To create a book which will enable others to guess each story character based on the description you write and the pictures you draw.

Steps:

1. Select the type of book you want to make from the book recipes on pages 59–61. Follow the instructions.
2. Decide how many characters you want to include from the story.
3. Create a cover and write your introduction (see examples on page 51) on the first page. Write information about each character on right-hand pages. Draw the characters on the left-hand pages.
4. Share your book with friends who have read the story. Can they guess the characters?

Guess the Character Book

Book cover

Guess
the
Character

by

Andy Meade

Introduction

Introduction
to
book

This is a guess the character book on "The Call of the Wild." Read the quote from the character and look on the back of the page for their name and picture.

right-side page

I'm the short-tempered dog who doesn't like people walking up to my blind side. My name has a hyphen in the middle. At first I didn't like Buck. He was always getting tangled in the lines and delayed all of us. But after I got used to him, I decided that he was O.K.

left-side page

Sol-Leks

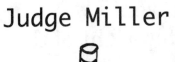

right-side page

I am the previous owner of Buck. He was a good dog, always following me wherever I went. I am also the judge around here. What is my name?

left-side page

Judge Miller

left-side page

I gotta whip dem' nuts ta get anyting' outa' dem. My name starts with an "H". Mercedies is my wife and John is my brother-in-law. I run the mail train. Who am I?

right-side page

Hans

Story Viewer

A Story Viewer is an interesting addition to any book presentation. Just change the story roll and the box can be used over and over to retell many different stories. Adult supervision is required for cutting.

Materials:
Large cardboard box
Exacto™ knife
Roll of white shelf paper
Masking tape
Paper towel tubes (2)
Markers

Goal:
To retell the story through a story box.

Steps:
1. Cut a large rectangular screen in the box front.
2. Using the shelf paper, create a story frame (a bit larger than the screen) that includes the book title and an illustration and description of each key event.
3. Draw and cut a hole in the top-left and top-right of the box. Do the same in the bottom of the box (see example on page 53).
4. Place the tube ends into the holes.
5. Tape each end of your story roll to a tube.
6. Set the story box on the edge of a desk so the tubes turn easily.
7. Slowly turn the tubes to tell the story.

Story Viewer Directions

Step 1

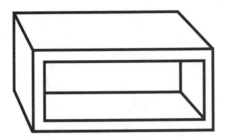

Turn the box on its side and cut a large rectangle in the front. This will become your story viewer screen.

Step 2

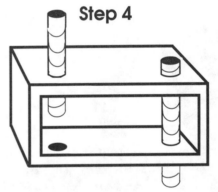

Create story frames slightly larger than the screen on the shelf paper. The title frame is first and the story events come next.

Step 3

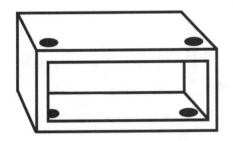

Draw and cut two holes in the top and bottom at the front of the screen.

Step 4

Place the tube ends into the holes.

Step 5

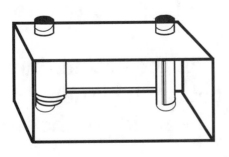

Tape each end of your story roll to a tube.

Step 6

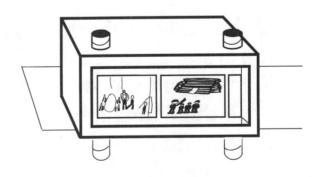

Set the box on the edge of a desk so the tubes turn easily.

Story Sack Retell

A Story Sack is great fun for all ages. The sack can also be used to collect ideas for the plot of a story the young author is writing.

Materials:
Markers/pencils
Page 62
Scissors
Glue

Goal:
To share key items as you re-tell a story to your friends.

Steps:
1. Copy the pattern on page 62 and cut out the pieces.
2. Write the story title, author and your name in one of the large panels. Decorate the panels with story items.
3. Make a list of story items which represent key events. Make and/or collect items which will help you to retell the story.
4. Fold the cut out story sack pattern on the dotted lines. Glue the end pieces and the sack bottom together.
5. Tape or glue the cut out handle to the inside of the two small panels.
6. Retell your story to friends using the items from your story sack.

Story Sack Directions

Steps 1 and 2

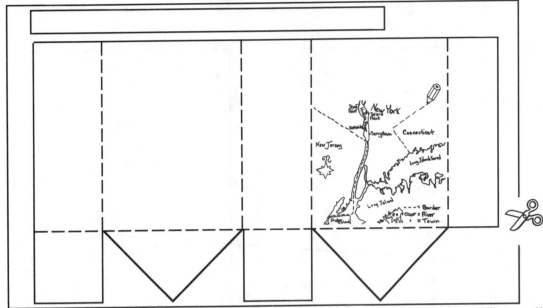

Copy the pattern on page 62 and cut the pieces out. Write the story title, author, and your name in one large panel. Decorate the panels with story items.

Step 3

Make and/or collect items to fit in your story sack that represent important events.

Steps 4 and 5

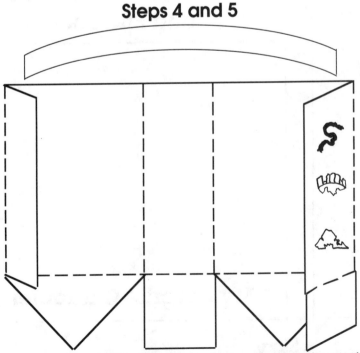

Fold on the dotted lines and glue the ends and the sack bottom together. Glue on the handle,

Sample

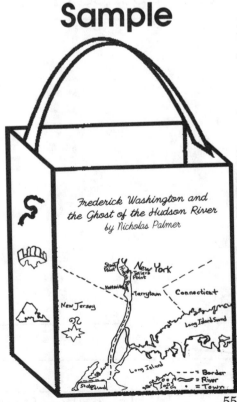

Frederick Washington and the Ghost of the Hudson River
by Nicholas Palmer

_____

_____

_____

[blank box]

This happened in the **middle**...

_____

_____

_____

[blank box]

This happened in the **beginning**...

This happened in the **end**...

[blank box]

My Beginning, Middle, and End Book

[blank box]

My Favorite Character

Story:_____

My name:_____

Project Recipes

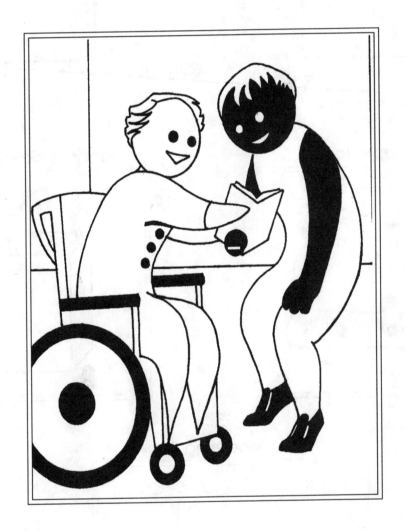

Chapter 4

Chapter Contents

Card Book

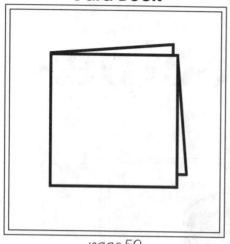

Sewn Book

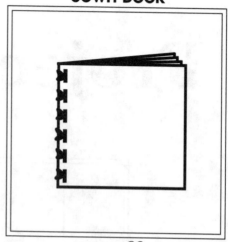

Shape Book

Story Sack Pattern

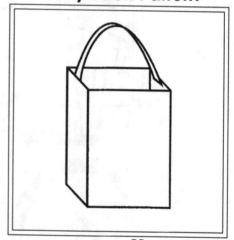

Modeling Clay

Card Book

Step 1

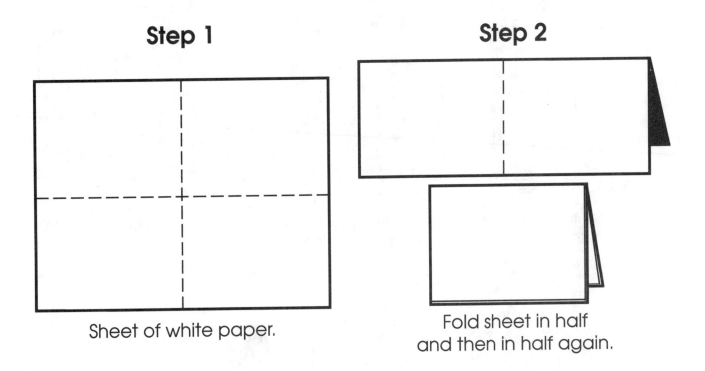

Sheet of white paper.

Step 2

Fold sheet in half
and then in half again.

Step 3

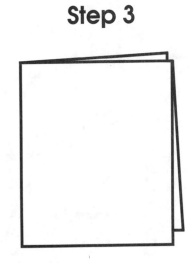

Turn the paper around so it opens
like a card.

Sewn Book

☑ **Materials:**
- ❑ 2 tagboard pieces (5 1/2-by-4 1/4 inches)
- ❑ Plastic sewing needle
- ❑ Pencil/markers
- ❑ Yarn or cord
- ❑ Paper
- ❑ Hole punch

Steps 1 and 2

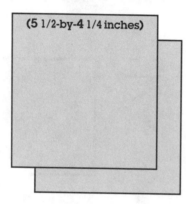

Fold paper two ways and
cut into fourths.

Step 3

(5 1/2-by-4 1/4 inches)

Cut two tagboard
pieces for the cover.

Step 4

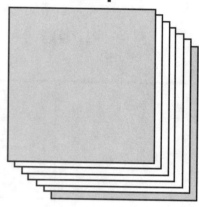

Place the covers above
and below the pages.

Step 5

Punch holes in the
stacked pieces.

Step 6

Cut a 33 1/2"
piece of yarn.

Step 7

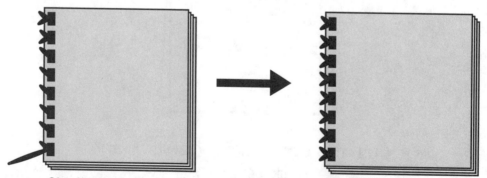

Starting at the bottom, loop yarn around the holes.
Continue looping from the top back down. Tie the loose ends.

Shape Book

Step 1

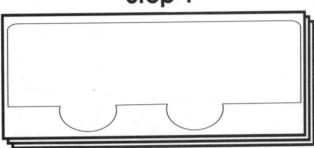

Decide how many pages you want in your book.
Draw a shape on construction paper.

Step 2

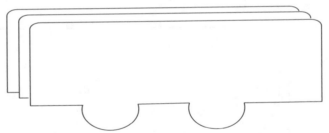

Cut out the cover and book pages using your design.

Step 3

Decorate your cover and complete your
book pages

Story Sack Pattern

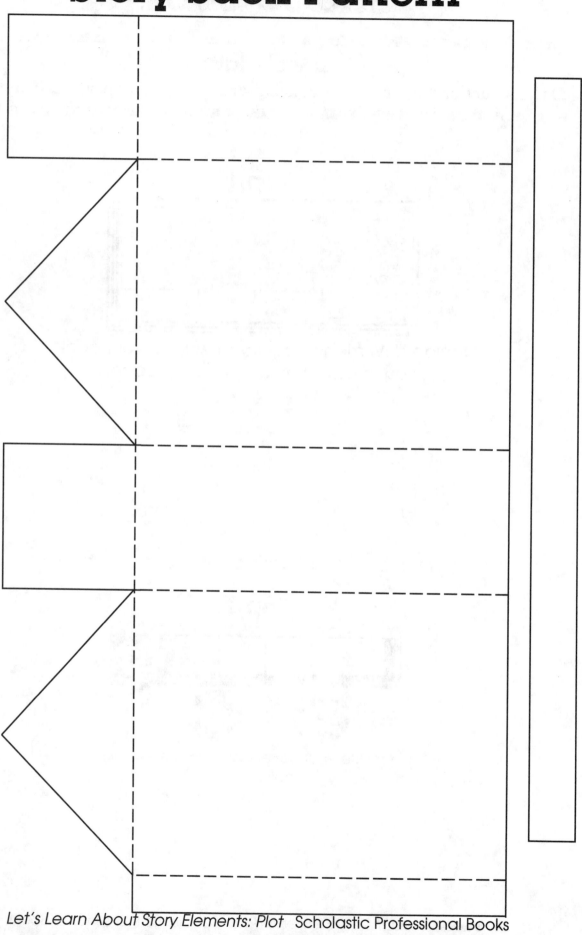

Let's Learn About Story Elements: Plot Scholastic Professional Books

Modeling Clay

Adult supervision required.

☑ Materials:

❏ Salt (1/2 cup) ❏ Cold Water (1/4 cup) ❏ Saucepan (1 medium)
❏ Hot Water (1/2 cup) ❏ Bowl/Spoons ❏ Measuring cup (1)
❏ Cornstarch (1/2 cup)

Step 1

Pour salt and hot water in a pan. Heat and stir until it boils.

Step 2

Pour the cornstarch in a bowl. Add cold water and stir.

Step 3

Add the cornstarch mixture to the boiling water. Stir it vigorously.

Step 4

Cook mixture over low heat, stirring continuously until it is stiff. Then let it cool.

Step 5

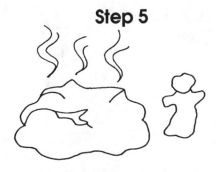

Knead clay until it's smooth. Create shapes out of it.

Step 6

Let shapes dry 1-2 days and paint them.

Let's Learn About Story Elements: Plot Scholastic Professional Books

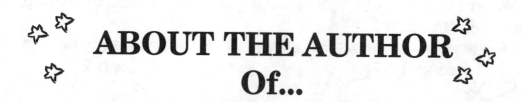

ABOUT THE AUTHOR
Of...

**BOOK-WRITE
BEYOND BOOK REPORTS
GREAT GRAPHIC ORGANIZERS
LET'S LEARN ABOUT STORY ELEMENTS: CHARACTER
LET'S LEARN ABOUT STORY ELEMENTS: SETTING**

Michelle O'Brien-Palmer

Michelle received her undergraduate and graduate degrees from the University of Washington. Her career in educational curriculum development and design spans twenty years.

Michelle works with students and teachers in five to six different classrooms throughout the school year as she writes each of her books. Children and classroom teachers always play an integral role in the creation of her books and music.

*•Educational Workshops and Inservices
•School Assemblies and Workshops
•Educational Consultation*

MicNik Publications, Inc. • P.O. Box 3041
Kirkland, Washington 98083
(425) 881-6476